ISBN: 9781494287733

Printed in the U.S.A.

New Eyes for Annie

I would like to thank the many people at Take My Paw Rescue, not only for saving this wonderful girl's life, but also for their friendship and the phenomenal work that they do saving so many lives and finding those animals their loving, forever families. Bonnie, Phil, Mary, Judy, John, Carol, and the many others that make Take My Paw Rescue the huge success that they are, thank you.

I would also like to thank Amanda Ward for her love and care of Annie. She loved you as much as you loved her! And my partner and BFF, Cheryll Gottschalk, for her part in fostering Annie, and for always being my BFF! (Love you, pal!)

And most of all, I would like to thank Cindy for giving Annie her purrfect, loving and forever home. I wish you both the happiest of lives, and my best wishes for a very long, loving and healthy life together!

New Eyes for Annie

My Name is Annie

It was April of 2012 when the people that I loved took me to a very scary place. I was supposed to have an operation so that I couldn't have kittens of my own. I was just three months old, but somehow I knew that my life was about to change.

The Very Scary Place

They said it was called a shelter. There was a doctor there who checked me all over. He felt my tummy, he checked my teeth and ears. Then he looked very closely into my eyes.

He talked to my people about taking me to another doctor because my eyes were cloudy looking. I knew it was hard to see, but I just thought that was the way it was supposed to be. Then my people said something that made me very sad. They said, "Just put her down". I didn't know what that meant, but when the doctor didn't put me on the floor, I knew that it wasn't good.

Life at the Shelter

The doctor refused to do whatever it was that my people wanted him to do, and instead had them sign a piece of paper so that I could stay with him at the shelter. I didn't want to stay there. I wanted to go home! I couldn't believe that they didn't want me anymore, just because I couldn't see very well!

The doctor picked me up and took me to a big room. The room had cages in it, and the doctor put me in one of the cages. I was so scared, but the doctor petted me and told me that everything would be okay. He gave me food and water, and a warm blanket to cuddle.

<u>A Safe Place to Go</u>

While I was at the shelter, I had my operation and got some shots to keep me healthy. I wasn't at the shelter very long before a group called Take My Paw Rescue took me from the shelter and gave me to a lady named Erin. Erin took me to another lady named Amanda, who took great care of me. She played with me and gave me tons of love! And I loved her, too.

Amanda had two cats of her own. Fluffy was very old and didn't pay much attention to me, and Cali did not like me at all! Cali would pick on me and try to start fights with me, but I still loved being with Amanda. Sometimes she had friends over and we had lots of fun! There were so many laps to cuddle up on and people to pet me and love me. I was very happy at Amanda's.

The Eye Doctor

One beautiful sunny day, Erin came to Amanda's to pick me up. She put me in a carrier and then into her car. I didn't like it in that carrier. I wanted to cuddle! I cried and cried, and I reached through the carrier door and pawed at her leg. Finally, she stopped the car and let me out of the carrier. I cuddled in her lap for the long drive to the doctor who would look at my eyes.

We got to the doctor early, so we just cuddled a lot while we waited in the car. I stood up and gave Erin a few kisses, and she gave me kisses, too. Then I fell asleep in her lap.

After a while, we went into the doctor's office. The doctor was very nice, and checked me all over. Like the other doctor, he felt my tummy and checked my teeth and ears. And then he looked deep into my eyes.

He put orange dye in my eyes and looked at them again. When he was done, he told Erin that all I had was something called a herpes virus and just needed some eye drops for a while! Hooray!

After the appointment, we drove that long drive back to Amanda's house, and I slept in Erin's lap the whole time. I was very tired.

The Day I Met Cindy

I stayed at Amanda's for about two more months and had a lot of fun. She was very nice to me and took great care of me!

After a while, I moved to Cheryll's house. There were so many things to play with! I got in trouble a lot, though. I guess I wasn't supposed to play with all of those things on her shelves! I was only at Cheryll's for about two weeks when Erin called her and said that she had found the perfect home for me! It was so confusing! Every time I thought I was home, I had to move again!

Erin came to pick me up, and gathered all of my things. Into the car we went and drove away. She took me to a place where we met a woman named Cindy.

Erin took me out of the car and put me in Cindy's arms. Oh, this felt so good and so right! Somehow I knew this was where I was supposed to be.

A Home to Call My Own

I already loved Cindy, and I had just met her! She loved me, too. I could feel it in my heart. She held me close, kissed and hugged me. She got in her car, her boyfriend in the driver's seat, and we drove away.

It was a very long car ride and took most of the day to get to my new home. I mostly slept in Cindy's lap. When we got to Cindy's house, I was very curious and looked in every room. It was a beautiful home, and I hoped so much that I would get to stay this time.

There were so many toys to play with, and I had so much fun! I had lots of little toy mice to play with, and they are my favorite! There was a tunnel, a cat tree, a scratch post, and my own bed! Everything I had always wanted! All for me!

Forever At Last

As time went on, I met more of Cindy's family. They were all so nice, and the kids are so fun to play with. And when Cindy is sitting at her desk working, I have my own little comfy place that I sleep so I can be near her. Oh, how I do love her! And the best part of all? I can *see* my new special mommy, too!

I love my new mommy, and everyone else who gave me my sight and a second chance at life.

Thank you, from the bottom of my heart.

Love,

Annie

Made in the USA
Lexington, KY
03 April 2018